Naomi Learns
the Importance of Sleep

By: Dr. Jonathan Kushnir

Illustrations: Nikola Aronova

Naomi Learns the Importance of Sleep
By: Dr. Jonathan Kushnir

Printed in the United States of America
First Printing, 2023

ISBN: 9798393252205

Please visit us online for more information.
Facebook: https://www.cbtails.com

Introduction to the Reading Parent

Sleep is a universal phenomenon for all humans and animals. However, explaining what sleep is and why it is essential, even for adults, is not simple. This book aims to help children and parents learn about sleep in a fun and engaging way through the story of Naomi, a curious child who wants to know more about sleep.

In this book, Naomi learns about the concept of sleep, the benefits of a good night's sleep, and the consequences of not sleeping well. Her parents explain these concepts to her at bedtime, helping her better understand the importance of sleep.

This book aims to help parents explain the concept of sleep and its importance more easily to their children. The explanations are embedded in the story, making it easier for parents to engage their children in discussions about sleep. We hope that this will encourage children to develop healthy sleep habits.

The principles described in this book are based on years of research in the field of children's sleep.

Dr. Jonathan Kushnir

4

One evening, not long after the sun went down, Naomi's mommy and daddy told her that it was time to go to bed.

"Why do I have to go to bed?" Naomi asked.
"Sleep is really important for children,"
Daddy replied.

6

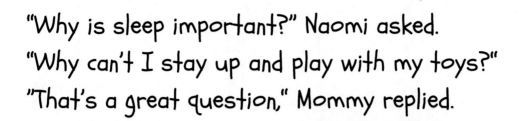

"Why is sleep important?" Naomi asked.
"Why can't I stay up and play with my toys?"
"That's a great question," Mommy replied.

7

Daddy and Mommy sat down on the sofa,
and Naomi climbed in between them.
Then they started to explain.

8

"Everybody in the world sleeps!
Grown-ups sleep, kids sleep, and
even children in faraway places like England
and France go to sleep too."

"Children all over the world,
like in Africa and China,
also go to sleep."

"Kids in Mexico and Brazil
also go to sleep!"

"Even animals sleep. Hippos, lions, and zebras all need sleep too!"

"Dolphins also sleep, but did you know
they sleep with one eye open?"

"But why do we all need to sleep?"
Naomi asked. "I'll explain," Mommy replied.
"When you sleep, your body gets to rest
and regain the energy you need for
the next day."

"When you sleep, your brain gets to rest and sort through all the things you learned and thought about during the day."

"Sleep also helps keep your body healthy by getting rid of germs!"

"Sleep even helps you grow!" Mommy said.
"I want to grow big and strong", said Naomi.

17

Daddy and Mommy said, "When you sleep,
your body goes through four different parts.
These parts keep repeating in a cycle all night long!".

"In the first part of sleep, you start
to feel tired and eventually fall asleep.
But if you need to wake up,
it's pretty easy to do so!"

19

"In the second stage of sleep, your heartbeat slows down, and your body gets cooler. It's really tough to wake up during this part of sleep. And if you do manage to wake up, you might feel a little confused and sleepy."

20

"In the third part of sleep, your breathing slows down and your body becomes really relaxed. That's when you are in your deepest sleep!"

21

"In the fourth stage, your eyes move around under your closed eyelids, and this is when you have dreams. It's also harder to move your body during this stage."

22

"What happens after the fourth part?" Naomi asked. "You keep going through the parts again and again until it's morning," Daddy replied.

"What happens if I don't sleep?" Naomi asked.

"That's a great question too," Mommy replied. "If you don't sleep, you'll feel tired and grumpy during the day."

"And if you don't sleep, it can be harder to pay attention and listen to your teacher, Daddy, or me," Mommy added.

26

"You might even become clumsy, and that can make it hard to play with your friends or toys," Daddy explained.

Just then, Naomi let out a big yawn.
"I want to go to bed. I need to sleep,"
she said.

Mommy and Daddy picked up Naomi and carried her to her room. They tucked her into bed with her favorite plush toy.

As Naomi snuggled under the covers,
she thought about why sleep was so important.
She remembered all the grown-ups, children,
and animals around the world who sleep too.

And she fell asleep.

31

Dr. Kushnir
Clinical Psychologist

Dr. Jonathan Kushnir is a clinical psychologist, an expert and an instructor in Cognitive Behavior Therapy, accredited by the European Association for Behavioral Therapies. After completing his Ph.D. in clinical psychology in Israel and a research fellowship in the U.S, he has successfully treated thousands of children and adults suffering from emotional anxieties for over a decade. His insightful articles on the subject have been published in top scientific - peer-reviewed journals.

Made in the USA
Coppell, TX
19 October 2024

38937424R00021